Dustmop Devotionals

by Katharine Wool Parrish

PRESENTED TO

_____

_____

_____

FROM

_____

_____

_____

Bite-sized meditations
for every harried homemaker.

MERIDIAN®
SLIMLINES

This edition is published by special arrangement with and permission of Star Books, Inc., Wilson, NC.

All scripture quotations are taken from the New American Standard Bible © The Lockman Foundation.

Grateful acknowledgement is made for permission to reprint "First Flight" from *Living With Teenagers* © 1980 by The Sunday School Board of the Southern Baptist Convention, Nashville, TN. Used by permission.

Much of the materials were originally published also as *Dustmop Devotionals* © 1986 by Katharine Parrish and Star Books, Inc., and used by permission. All rights reserved.

This completely revised edition © 1990 by Meridian Publishing, Grand Rapids, MI. All rights reserved.

M9 Slimline Gift Edition   ISBN 0-529-06785-4
M35 Large Gift Edition   ISBN 0-529-07127-4

Book and cover design by Gayle Raymer

Published with World Bible Publishers
Printed in the United States of America

Divorce Tangle	54
Upswing	57
First Flight	58
Mother's Window	60
The Pondering	61
Breakfast Miracle	63
Laundry Room	66
Blurred Vision	69
Dangerous Roar	71
Visiting Day	73
Reclaimed	76
More Than Enough	77
Constant Reminder	79

Contents

Acknowledgements 5
Introduction 7
Dustmop Devotional 9
Perfect Pickles 11
Dedication 13
Healing Radiance 14
Mournful Lament for Monday 17
Same Old Song 18
Hush-A-Bye 20
Sweet Fragrance 22
Incense 24
Tattletale 25
Tumbled Priorities 27
Compassion 29
Bottled 31
Forget It 32
Nothing Hidden 34
A Super Day 36
Snowflake Dance 38
"Won't Daddy Be Proud?" 41
So What? 43
Sunday Shoes 46
Identity Crisis 48
Mending Basket 50
Darning Thread 52

Acknowledgements

Thanks for this book go to my mother, whose enduring faith proved it was possible;

To my husband, Jerry, God's gracious covering and provider, with much gratitude for the freedom of time and understanding which he offered in love;

To praying friends who believed in the ministry of Dustmop long before it became a reality; and

Most of all, to Sarah, Jeannie, Jim, Mary, Julie, and Tim, who allowed me to tell their stories.

Introduction

One winter afternoon I read a book that made me weep. It also made me pray. I wept with gratitude for the little ones in my constant care, and prayed for strength and love to be the mother God wanted for them.

I also prayed that, one day when I had a breather from diapers and carpools, He would enable me to write a book that would inspire and encourage mothers. God answers prayer! Now my children—Sarah, Jeannie, Jim, Mary, John in Heaven, Julie, and Tim are grown and almost grown. And here's the book!

During the preparation of these devotionals, I have prayed for each reader, knowing how lovingly God's Spirit can speak to your heart.

Dustmop Devotional

Come, let us worship and bow down;
let us kneel before the Lord our maker,
For he is our God,
and we are the people of his pasture,
and the sheep of his hand.
Psalm 95:6,7

I seem to be always talking to God from the floor. This morning, I find myself kneeling beside the grimy bathtub, brush in hand and prayers in mind. My best thinking times seem to come when I'm here—or down under the bed with the dustmop, sweeping unmatched socks and parts of games from under the couch, or unclogging the refrigerator drain.

It sounds crazy, but I find myself worshiping, settling problems, realizing the answers to yesterday's prayers, remembering people who need God's love and my petitions.

Perhaps the old Renaissance monks, who spent their lives and devotion doing the most menial tasks on their knees, knew a secret for this sort of working meditation.

The ordinary day of a mother-homemaker doesn't allow for much set-aside time for leisurely thinking or self-development. I have a tendency to drop off to sleep whenever I sit still for longer than five minutes in a quiet place. It's handy the way my conversation with the Lord somehow fits the rhythm of mop and sponge and dustcloth.

I don't always like this work, the mother-jobs of changing beds, wiping up sticky spills, rinsing dirty diapers, loading the clothes dryer, repairing bicycle chains, or cleaning out toy boxes and clothes closets. Daily chores aren't always fun.

But neither was the work of those old monks who were simply obedient.

Lord, that's what you want of me, isn't it? Simple obedience in the ministry to which you have called me in my home.

I'm sure there will still be many times of complaining about all the work here, Lord. Many days I will feel misused and unappreciated. But just now I'm kneeling–by the sparkling clean bathtub–worshiping the kind of love that can lift me into glory by the simple obedience and lowly service of motherhood.

Perfect Pickles

*Therefore you are to be perfect,
as your Father is perfect.*
Matthew 5:48

To me, the best thing about July is fresh peaches at the market. They look and smell so good and I've just bought a whole bushel!

On the way home I've been thinking how much the family would enjoy pickled peaches along about November.

As I unload the soft, rosy fruit onto the back porch table, there seem to be more peaches than when I started—and all of them must be sorted, peeled, and preserved.

The ones that smell best are too ripe for anything but eating and enjoying. I put them into the refrigerator for juicy snacks, peach ice cream, and maybe a pie for supper.

Into another bowl I put the fruit that's still too hard. In a day or two it will be good for eating too.

Some of the other peaches look good at first glance, but as I inspect them I find dark, soft spots from rough handling. These must be refrigerated too.

The largest bowl holds only perfect peaches. These I will cook and seal in hot jars with spices that will make them a treat for our winter Sunday table.

Lord, it seems funny, but I can see myself in these peaches. Maybe it's because I'm a little tired of peeling, sorting, and of fighting flies in this heat.

I can be a soft, sweet Christian, but I won't last long.

If I'm hard and stiff, I can be useful after I had time to ripen and get some flavor.

Even if I have some hurt, bruised places, there is a lot of good that can be salvaged.

But you said perfect, didn't you, Lord? That means being just what you designed me to be, for your own table. Not too soft, nor too hard, nor blemished with hurt places. But I can't be this perfect fruit without your help, Lord.

I have to let you ripen, trim, peel, simmer and seal with your Holy Spirit.

Thank you, Lord Jesus, for the tender, careful way you prepare me for your own perfect use.

Thank you, too, Lord, that this summer's peach pickles are all packed in jars, looking clear and appetizing. That's a lot of work and it's done!

Dedication

The sun of early summer is on my back.
I pin—one after the other—
Shirts and towels on the clothesline.
My little one trails his pull-toy
Through the grass, and stoops
To have soft conversation
With the ants who live there.

Lord, why can't it always be this way?
The seasons give their gentle prophecy—
Lacy whiteness by the road heralds
Fat, black berries to come.
A bird biting a scrap of string
Hurries to nest.
Heavy buds burst into leaves that
Cast figured shade on soft new green,
And dusty bulbs fulfill their autumn promise
In rainbow brightness by the porch.

We walk in the quiet lane,
As I have walked with his siblings,
These marching years.
We kneel to worship at the cluster
Of dainty bluets under a great oak.
I pray again, "Lord, make his
   growing-up good,
And keep him close to you as he is today,
In this four-year old fellowship."

Healing Radiance

*They looked to him and were radiant,
and their faces shall never be ashamed.*

Psalm 34:5

It was terribly embarrassing. In the middle of the large department store, my darling four-year-old daughter was screaming hysterically. I had no idea why, until I saw the man with his crutches. He had a cast on one leg, and was leaning against a counter.

Sarah didn't calm down until we were in the car and headed home. What was the matter with her? She was usually a happy, reasonable child—until she saw someone with a bandage, braces, crutches, or a cast.

On the way home, we stopped to see a favorite aunt who wore a brace on one leg. I dreaded the visit, because, in the past, Sarah had always screamed and refused to get out of the car at Aunt Jean's house.

Leaving her in the car and telling her I would be right back, I went inside and told my aunt about the department store incident, because I believed there was a connection between that and Sarah's fear at her house.

Aunt Jean knew exactly what to do.

"You stay in the house," she said to me. "I'll go out and get Sarah."

I was amazed when, in a few minutes, the two came in holding hands and smiling.

"What on earth did you do?" I asked.

"Remember the automobile accident you two were in, when she was just a baby?" she said, beginning to explain.

"Yes, but that was before she could remember."

"I know, but the fear and pain have been in her subconscious mind all these years. That's why she gets so upset when she sees people who seem to be hurting."

We sat down on her comfortable screened porch and she went on.

"But how did you get her not to be afraid of you?"

"I just told her to look at my face," Aunt Jean replied.

"And I told her she doesn't have to worry about the brace—it only helps me to walk better. I'll always be smiling, for her." She looked down at the happy child whose eyes were fixed on her face.

The lesson worked. There were no more hysterical scenes, and no more refusals to visit our favorite aunt.

Lord, your body was broken for me. I can't bear to look on it without great pain and fear. But when I look up—at your face—I see shining there the love that went to Calvary for me, the joy of eternal life, and the peace of belonging to you. There is healing for things I don't understand—like the subconscious trauma of Sarah's experience as an infant—and for the frightening things I do understand in my world. Keep me looking at the beauty in your face, Lord, that I may be radiant too.

Mournful Lament for Monday

The trash cans all are full today,
And drooping on the floor
Are sodden mounds of towels piled
Against the bathroom door.

There's Sunday's great and funny news
And half-filled cups that lurk
Beneath the chairs that mark my path
To mop and broom—and work!

This solemn, empty day reflects
A weekend's recklessness,
And all my pride in motherhood
Seems raving helplessness.

But sogginess and stickiness,
Like pieces of my heart,
Can all be set aright again
With loving, patient art.

For this wrecked place is home, and so—
For all the mess they bring,
I give my thanks and praise, dear Lord,
For each teenager's thing.

Same Old Song

*Many a man proclaims his own loyalty,
but who can find a trustworthy man?*
Proverbs 20:6

We welcomed a new couple to our choir rehearsal last week. They have strong, lovely voices, and the choir sounded good with their added talent.

But they didn't show up on Sunday to help us with the difficult piece we'd practiced.

I was reminded of a story about a young, medieval monk and his visit to a wayside monastery. The monk had a glorious tenor voice, and when he sang the matins, the others gradually stopped singing just to listen to his round, sweet notes floating heavenward. At evensong, the same thing happened, and the story goes that God appeared in a dream to the old abbot that night.

"Why did I hear no singing at the worship services today?" he asked.

"Lord," replied the old man, "you must have heard the beautiful hymns. Our new brother lifted his voice to sing, and we fell silent, ashamed of our poor, cracking notes."

"I heard no hymns," insisted the Lord. "It is the praise of the heart I hear, and your hearts were silent this day. Your ears are not like my ears."

Lord, like the old monks, we sometimes tire of our own mediocre singing. To you, however, it is the praise of faithful hearts coming to sing, to worship, and to work for you Sunday by Sunday, day after day, that makes music in heaven. Help me to remember how precious to you is a faithful, serving, singing, heart—whether the notes are true or not.

Hush-A-Bye

*Surely I have composed and quieted my soul;
Like a weaned child
rests against its mother's breast;
my soul is quieted within me.*
Psalm 131:2

The baby's cry pierces the night, and I drag myself up from what must have been only a few minutes of sleep to discover that it's feeding time again. Even though Mary is our fourth, I'd forgotten how incessantly demanding a tiny baby can be.

I gather up the squalling, squirming bundle and we make our groping way to the living room and a comfortable rocker.

"Have I ever in your whole three-week life let you go hungry?" I scold the red-faced infant as I change a soggy diaper and try to wrap the receiving blanket around her feet.

"Hush, now. You'll wake the rest of the family."

In a few seconds, she is nestled against my breast, reaching, grabbing, finally sucking. Soon the small hands stop flailing and lie peacefully beside the tiny, busy mouth.

Anxiety has left the large brown eyes. Even in the darkened room, I see them smile in contentment and slowly close. I cover the little feet dangling from my hand, and settle into the rhythm of a soft, old lullaby.

Once again my child is satisfied. She is secure and relaxed in my arms.

As I lay her back in the crib and spread the quilt over her, I can't help crying tears of gratitude for this precious child, and the fulfillment I know in meeting her needs.

Crawling back into my own warm bed beside her proud, sleeping daddy, I know that, in the space of a few short hours, this time of satisfaction will be completely unremembered. She will be howling again, demanding until she is fed once more.

Lord Jesus, I'm just like this sweet Mary. I scream and grab, squirm and flail, when days get difficult around here. It seems more natural to cry out than to remember how you wonderfully met my needs just a short time ago—at the last feeding-time—when I found comfort in your loving presence.

Like Mary's squirming body, my soul needs quieting. Only as I come and feed on your Word am I nourished and finally satisfied. Forgive me, Father, for this short memory. Gather me into your arms, and my soul will again be composed and quieted at its mother's breast.

And, Lord, please remind me of all this the next time that little one splits open my night's sleep with her screams.

Sweet Fragrance

For we are a fragrance of Christ to God among those who are being saved.
2 Corinthians 2:15

My house smells good today! All the time my friend and I were talking, I enjoyed the sweetness of her perfume. It's a scent I'm not used to—probably a little too expensive for my purse, but sophisticated and lovely. The fragrance of her visit lingers long after the door has closed on her retreating figure.

When the children come in from school, they remark, "Smells good in here," and I remember times they were greeted with a different scent. How often I've tried to conceal the fact that I let the butterbeans boil over, or fried the bacon too long, or burned the cookies. Try as I might to pull the telltale odor out with the exhaust fan, or cover it with some fancy odor-eating spray, my family always knows. There's the twitching of noses, and the comment, "Sump'n'burn, Mom?"

There have also been good times, when the aroma of bread rising, or brownies baking, or the holiday turkey cooking welcomes the family to a loving home. I like to think those memories outweigh the times when the smoke alarm shrieks its tattletale warnings, and they all come running to investigate the latest disaster.

It does smell good today, Lord. It feels good too. My friend is a blessing, and her sweetness of spirit lasts even longer than the trace of her delicate perfume. I believe that's because she brought more than a new cologne. She brought "the fragrance of Christ," as we shared our hearts' joys and sorrows. The aroma of her compassion was like incense rising as we prayed together. Thank you Lord, for that kind of friend—who sits in my kitchen and makes it a sweet-smelling sanctuary.

Incense

Such fragrance is here, O my Lord,
As I walk with my small ones and talk
Just after the September rain.

Deep sweetness of fellowship comes
With touching the soft silkened seed
And watching its high, fragile flight.

The scent of bright maple and pine,
The red-berried dogwood that bows
To squishing-up mud by the road.

Delicious, O Lord, as your Word
Is this moment of golden-robed day
Shared with young hearts turned to you.

Tattletale

Whoever does not receive the kingdom of God like a child, shall not enter it at all.
Mark 10:15

It was early October and I walked with four-year-old John along our dusty road, feeling the warm sun on my back. We talked about the beauty of red, orange, and yellow leaves. Plucking long, feathery weeds along the ditch bank, we fashioned a fall bouquet for the dining-room table.

We shared, this sensitive son and I, our joy in the wonderful world God had made for us and spoke of the need to take good care of it. We watched a cardinal flash its brilliance against the sky and come to rest in the young maple in the vacant lot across the road.

It was happy chatter, but I had no idea how much he understood, until the next day. Pulling the car into the driveway after his morning at preschool, I heard a shrill, demanding, "Mama, look! Look at what that man's doin'!"

A tractor was pushing down the lovely maple tree in the vacant lot. We watched as the man got off the machine and placed a sign where the golden limbs had so recently reached toward the sun, offering shelter to the birds and shade to passersby. The sign advertised some duplexes that were being built on a neighboring street.

As we stared, John's young voice rang out, "I'm gonna' tell God!" Then he marched to his room, to do just that.

Lord, you must have been listening as this small one reported what he felt was a real sin. He knew you cared about his lovely world, and he knew that he could take his problem right to you. How simple his faith is. It must have been well-founded too. Within six months, the man whose crime John reported went bankrupt.

Thank you, Lord, for the faith of this child. Thank you also for the lesson he taught me. You are my loving Father and I can come straight to you with my concerns. You will hear and answer me as you heard and answered John—as long as my faith is simple and sure.

Tumbled Priorities

*But seek first his kingdom
and his righteousness;
and all these things shall be added to you.*
Matthew 6:33

When I walked into the office and heard, "You're almost late again, dear. You may be trying to do too much before you come to work," I wanted to go sit in the car and cry!

There wasn't time for that, so while I mixed paints and prepared table games, I tried to count up what I did before coming in to teach.

I remembered getting up before dawn, showering before my teenagers could get the shower, serving three different breakfasts to accommodate three different bus schedules, loading the washer and dryer, squeezing in prayers, taking a moment with my husband, making beds, washing dishes, feeding animals, passing out lunch money, checking on notes and snacks for school, and flossing my teeth while applying makeup.

Why did I think I could handle even a part-time job and home responsibilities too?

Lots of women "successfully combine"—or so I hear—the two careers. Maybe I just can't though. Maybe going back to work was a mistake.

After all this, I had to admit that the job was pure fun! As I welcomed children to the classroom and entered their wonderful world, saw trust and love in their eyes, I knew it was all worth it. When I heard, "I brought these flowers for you 'cause I love you, Teacher," shared the exultation of the youngster who discovered that he could complete a once-difficult task, and watched as a precious three-year-old began to interact with a new friend in a trusting relationship, I wanted to sing with them (and I did), "If you're happy and you know it, clap your hands!"

I had the wonderful, God-given feeling that I was doing what I was trained to do, and doing it well. I was molding young lives in a positive way, and that felt good.

Thank you Lord, for this fulfilling job. Help me to rearrange my priorities so that I take care of the important things at home. The children are big enough to do more than I think, and I'm big enough to let some things go once in a while. Thank you, also, for an understanding husband and boss!

Compassion

*He who did not spare his own Son,
but delivered him up for us all,
how will he not also with him
also freely give us all things?*
Romans 8:32

The gentle spring twilight warmed us as my husband and I drove home from the hospital to spend the night with our four older children. For two days we had stayed close by the bedside of four-year-old John, watching for the slightest movement or any sign at all that he sensed our presence with him. There was none. Through the long hours that followed a violent seizure, we had sought in vain to communicate with the child inside that unresponsive body.

Finally the doctors told us kindly that his brain had suffered too much damage. Only the machines were keeping the life processes going, and if John didn't begin breathing on his own within the next few hours, they would turn the machines off and let the little heart stop.

Straining as we had been for some sign of hope, Jerry and I finally admitted that our youngest, liveliest child had already gone from us to his heavenly home. Still I fought the anguish rising within me.

"I can't stand to see his little body broken, paralyzed by this awful sickness!" I cried out to God within the silence of my grief. As I wept, my mother heart accused, "God, how can you love us and let this happen?"

Jerry's grief mirrored my own. "Oh, I wish I could take his place," he said, as the tears splashed down his cheeks. "I love that little boy so much. Why can't I take the hurt for him?"

Then I heard another Voice. "I know that pain. I, too, watched a beloved Son suffer and die." There was so much love and sorrow in the words that I could hardly bear to listen as the Voice went on.

"I did it for you."

Lord God, you watched in pain beyond my imagining as your own Son suffered the awful anguish of sin for me. I am enfolded in comfort and peace, with the knowledge of that marvelous love.

Bottled

Safely in your keeping, Lord,
The grief of a year is put away.
And memories—even the bad ones—
Are eased, without pain,
Each sealed in its own fragrance.

You've been here, too, Lord,
In the searing time of giving up;
The empty anger that a child is gone;
The sweetness of holding small things
And wrapping them away.

Now the time for tears is past.
You never said there shouldn't be any
You only said you have a place for them.

Gracious Lord, only unthinkable love
Could cherish my grief
And refine it to joy.

Forget It

*And they were bringing children to him
as that he might touch them...*
Mark 10:13

It wouldn't have been so bad if the scout leader weren't also my friend. Our girls play together, go to school together, and now both of them are in Emily's junior troop.

"I think you had better talk with her about it before things get any worse." My friend's voice showed her concern. "I know you wouldn't want your daughter to do something like this, but all the facts point to her. I'm sorry to have to tell you, but I thought you'd want to know."

I thanked her, trying to sound sincere but calm (which I wasn't). Then I went back to the job of cleaning out the fireplace, and my tears spilled on the hearth as I remembered the painful conversation: *Money missing from the troop treasury. How could she? I have to do something. My child just can't grow up like this.*

Kneeling before the blackened hearth, I seemed to hear a Voice from deep within my soul.

"You can't do anything. Hand her over to me. Trust me completely for her life, or forget the whole business of professing your faith."

Could that be God speaking to me? Surely he expects me to work at rearing my children, and he knows how hard I try. What will people—people like her troop leader—think?

Still, it seems that I am hearing a clear message: "Trust me or forget it."

So here I am, Lord, on sooty hands and knees, this time offering my precious child to you. Show us both what should be said and done when she comes home today. I know I must trust you for the outcome of this whole thing, but it seems so difficult.

Then I remember the scriptures. Those Hebrew mothers—so long ago—brought their children to you because they knew it was the best assurance of happiness they could give them. I come as they did, bringing my own beautiful little girl, so that you may touch her as you did the children that day. I don't know how to make her life good, but I do know I can trust your love for both of us.

Thank you, Lord, for the reminder of that love. Thank you, too, that you will be here when she gets off the school bus.

Nothing Hidden

*But there is nothing covered up
that will not be revealed,
and nothing hidden that will not be known.*
Luke 12:2

There they were, all the family and in-laws gathered in my dining room for my first attempt at the annual Thanksgiving dinner. I was only a little nervous as I took the jellied cranberry salad from its mold and prepared it for the table. As I passed the refrigerator I saw it again, hanging there in blazing glory, the red ribbon from the state fair. I had been flabbergasted to find "CULINARY, 2ND PRIZE" on my blond brownies, but now the ribbon gave me a smug confidence that I was not such a bad homemaker after all.

The dinner went well until my three-year-old Jim finished his drumstick and slid from his chair while I was preparing to serve dessert. I heard one of his aunts squeal in mock surprise and say, "There's a little mouse under the table!"

I cringed, knowing what was coming next, but I was helpless to stop it.

"You wanna see a real mouse?" he asked, delighted. "Mama's got lots of 'em in her cabinets. I saw 'em!"

What does he need with such a marvelous memory? I fumed inwardly, my face red with embarrassment. Actually there had been only one mouse, weeks ago. But when I tried to explain, I only made matters worse. At least all the laughter at my expense warmed the family fellowship.

Lord, why do I ever try to hide anything? When company is coming, off comes the sagging, spotted couch cover. I add it to the pile in the already-stacked-up corner of the bedroom. Then, invariably, a guest asks to use the bedroom telephone. I shove bits of unfinished sewing, strewn toys, and unfolded laundry into a closet or cabinet, which turns out to be the very place where someone looks for napkins or games. Truly have you said, "There is nothing hidden that shall not be made known."

Lord, you alone know what's stuffed in the corners and closets of my life. When I dress up to sing in the choir or to attend a meeting, people might be fooled by how I look on the outside. But you made me, and you patiently work with what's inside, that which needs to be cleaned out, sorted, or discarded.

So clean me up, Lord. Empty me of what is not the best. Make me straight and neat, from the inside out. Like a freshly cleaned room with sparkling windows, I want to be open so your Spirit can shine through.

A Super Day

*For we are his workmanship,
created in Christ Jesus for good works,
which God prepared before hand that we
should walk in them.*

Ephesians 2:10

This was one terrific day! For once, I even feel peaceful about spills, quarrels, and frantically busy schedules. The lady in the store admired my children (they were behaving a little better than usual) and praised me for being a good Christian mother. At the time there seemed no reason to be anything but proud.

It's so easy to witness when I'm recognized as a "good" person. I can smile at my children when they're like this, and everything appears beautifully under control. I'm happy to be my Lord's disciple, as long as I can live in luxurious limelight.

Why can't I always feel like this? Why do I ever have to handle teenage temperaments and sibling tantrums, and plumbing problems?

Lord, that's the whole story of the Christian life, isn't it? It's how I behave in the difficult times that counts. It's the way I rely on your strength when mine goes out with the disintegrating garbage bag. It really doesn't matter how I look to other people—only that I keep on looking to you for strength to cope beautifully with all the spills, breakdowns, sibling quarrels, and my own selfishness.

Thank you, Lord Jesus, that you care about my everydays. And thank you, too, for that nice lady who doesn't know me very well, and said all those flattering things.

Snowflake Dance

And she gave birth to her first-born son; and she wrapped him in (baby) cloths, and laid him in a manger.

Luke 2:7

It seemed to me just one large inconvenience. The snow began early in the afternoon, just a week before Christmas, and soon the roads were covered with a white, slippery blanket. Anxiously I watched, wondering, *Can we get to church for cantata rehearsal tonight? Will school be cancelled tomorrow?* Memories of last winter's muddy boot tracks, crunched-up popcorn on the rug, and soggy caps and mittens drying everywhere began to haunt me.

But there was a celebration going on at the big family room window.

"Thank you, God," Mary's four-year-old voice was singing. Seven-year-old Jim's eyes were wide. "Look how big the flakes are—and so soft!"

Mary was jumping up and down. "It's sticking to the trees!" she shrilled. "It's decorating that old pine tree for Christmas!"

For a moment they were quiet, watching. Then I heard Mary's whisper. "Thanks for praying for snow, Jim. You did good. Thanks a lot, God."

That's all you want, isn't it, Lord? The simple, uncluttered faith and heartfelt thanks of little children. They prayed for snow. You sent it. They thanked you for it. The radio's weatherman is totally confused, but they aren't. How do any of us know this weather wasn't simply the answer to a child's prayer of faith?

The children are right, Lord. You do everything beautifully. As I venture with them into this cold wonder-world, fat, wet flakes kiss my nose and settle for a moment on my warm woolen scarf. I can see your fingerwork in the delicate edging of each old dry leaf and slender pine needle. Even the dusty weeds by the roadside are dressed in instant beauty and grace. The quiet settling around us speaks to me of your peace.

I can't help but think of Bethlehem, and the quiet way you came into our grimy old world. It was those with childlike faith who came to welcome you at a crude manger where slept love and hope, who sat at your feet in Bethany, who climbed into your lap for hugs, and who rejoiced in the tomb-angel's message.

Forgive my sins of worry and complaining, Lord. I praise you for the beauty around me, and for the fun of sharing it with these little ones.

And, Lord, remind me of this praise when I'm

mopping up from muddy boots, cleaning popcorn from the rug, and hanging soggy mittens and caps somewhere to dry.

"Won't Daddy Be Proud?"

*For it is God who is at work in you,
both to will and to work for his good pleasure.
Philippians 2:13*

Archella the cat prowled in and out of closets and cabinets for two days before she finally settled, that afternoon, in a corner under the den bookshelves. Delighted, the children—who had followed her around all this time—brought soft cloths for her nest, and took turns keeping watch. It was almost bedtime when we heard the first sad cries. Our pet was in pain, and would soon be giving birth. Eight-year-old Jim sat close by and stroked her gently.

"It's okay, Archie. You're gonna be a good mama." Then he looked at me, anxiety in his brown eyes. "She sounds so bad. Do you think she'll be okay, Mom?"

"Sure," I answered with only a bit of hesitation. It was my first kitten delivery too.

The labor was long. We ate supper in snatches, as Jim and five-year-old Mary kept their midwife-vigil. Finally, Jim called excitedly from the corner. "One's comin' out! C'mere, everybody!" We forgot bedtime as we hovered over the laboring mother. One, two, three, four tiny slimy babies emerged. Archella, purring loudly, licked each one to soft, furry life, and we watched them searching blindly for their first meal.

What a beautiful lesson about God's care of his creatures! I thought, as we talked softly about what had happened.

Suddenly, Mary's exuberance exploded. "Oh, Jim," she cried, "didn't we do a good job? Won't Daddy be proud of us?"

But their daddy, who arrived home about that time, was anything *but* proud of all those kittens. He only tolerated Archella because he hated having mice around the place. The idea of five felines under foot didn't really make him happy. He loved Jim and Mary, and because they loved the cat he endeavored to share the excitement of their first birthing experience.

Lord Jesus, I'm so much like these excited children. I decide what will please you, and then expect you to be proud of the job I do. I'm so busy planning, meeting, and working that I never hear your instructions, never know your preferences.

Thank you, Lord, that you yourself are at work within me, to help me to do what you want. Teach me to listen, Lord, and to accomplish something you can truly be proud of.

So What?

*Finally, brethren, whatever is true,
whatever is honorable, whatever is right,
whatever is pure, whatever is lovely,
whatever is of good repute,
if there is any excellence
and if anything worthy of praise,
let your mind dwell on these things.*

Philippians 4:8

This morning we went to visit a new family in our neighborhood. My seven-year-old Jim looked around at the immaculate apartment and stated flatly, "Our house ain't never been this clean, Mama." There was no criticism, no joking—just a statement of fact.

The lady of the house was embarrassed and I was mortified, until we got home.

I looked around at the home I love, and thought, *What if my house isn't shiny-clean like hers?* My eyes went from a film of dust on the coffee table to a pile of books, to littered toys, and stacks of school papers. Laundry in the basket and mending on the shelf are all waiting for attention.

All these things speak of a busy, children-filled home. *This house is full of treasure,* it occurs to me. *It's cluttered by love and dreams.*

A ragged daffodil beside the kitchen window reminds me of twelve-year-old Sarah's sadness at any suffering thing. Of times when she wept and prayed for beauty that was hurt. The flower was already a little droopy when she brought it in, but to me it's still beautiful.

Nine-year-old Jeannie's room is a mess again. There, in the midst of books, dolls, and scrambled bedcovers, is a thing of loveliness—a ceramic tray. Molded and decorated with love and talent, it's to be a gift for someone. It speaks of her eagerness to share her day with its disappointments and joys. I can almost hear her high, delighted squeal when she's happy. Does she know how I treasure these and her growing beauty, even when I fuss about the messy room?

Jim is the one who is always taking something apart. His room is littered with models and parts of things he's investigating. Jars and dishes hold weird, smelly experiments. If I don't squelch his curiosity about God's world by complaining, it could lead to wonderful things.

Mary's room is the only neat one. I am reminded of her special caring ability as I see the placement of a special doll and her stuffed animals on the bed. At four, she's so much fun, making us laugh at her and ourselves with her saucy manner and her growing vocabulary which is sometimes incorrectly used.

Lord, you and I know I could be a more conscientious housekeeper. Keep me, though, from worrying about neatness when the clutter is important. Teach me too, Lord, to appreciate the growing needs of these children, and not to be so concerned about what other people think.

Sunday Shoes

*Let your light shine before men in such a way
that they may see your good works,
and glorify your Father who is in heaven.*

Matthew 5:16

Just look! That child has given away her brand-new shoes!

Four-year-old Julie and her friend were playing in the back yard, and I heard the conversation.

"You wanna pair of new shoes? I got some you can have," my Julie began.

"Yeah, them's shiny ones. I like 'em!" answered her friend.

I heard all that, but I never dreamed my child would give away the shoes we had just bought for her. I suppose her friend didn't have shoes as nice as those. Neither does Julie—now. They were to be her Sunday shoes for a long time to come. We just can't afford to buy her any more. What will I do? She has only those worn-out tennis shoes to wear with her little ruffled dresses.

Actually, she was only doing what she had been taught. We told her God said to be kind and share what we have. We even told her that we must be willing to give away something we want, so that others may have what they need. But we didn't mean this!

Lord, you did mean this though, didn't you? You meant that if someone needs anything we have, brand new or not, we should give it away.

My little girl understands more about your unselfish love than I do. Julie's light is shining in the eyes of her happy friend, who is proudly wearing the patent leather slippers. My child's good works are showing, and she brings glory to you as I never could with all my Sunday school teaching and committee chairing.

Thank you, Lord, for this wonderful bargain— a lesson from my little one, for the price of a pair of shoes.

Identity Crisis

*For our citizenship is in heaven,
from which also we eagerly wait for a Savior,
the Lord Jesus Christ.*
Philippians 3:20

"Thank you very much." We bowed and smiled, hoping our Korean hosts would know what we meant. It was for us a gala evening —the annual "Korea Night" at a local university.

We had been invited to share the gourmet seven-course dinner and the entertainment that followed, consisting of native dances, songs, and games.

In that sea of faces, ours seemed to be the only non-Oriental ones. Little children dressed like keepsake dolls played among parents who chatted excitedly. The costumes of the adults were dazzling, their dancing filled with meaning and grace. The music was haunting and exquisitely lovely. Though we could understand nothing they spoke or sang, we were grasping the deep sense of pride these charming people have in their homeland. For our adopted child, himself Korean, we coveted this pride, and were really enjoying the warmth of being honored guests, until...

Six-year-old Timmy, not at all awed by the grandeur and grace of the occasion, announced loudly, "Lots of Chinese people here!"

(Embarrassment, thy name is parenthood!)

Seeking unsuccessfully to cover his outburst, I asked sweetly "Timmy, where are you from?"

Suddenly all those beautiful Korean faces turned toward this boisterous child with the straight black hair and eyes of slanted velvet. He marched through them, proudly announcing, "Me, 'merican!" and led his red-faced family to the door.

Lord, we too bear allegiance to another Kingdom. Make us as proud of that Kingdom as Timmy is of his adopted homeland.

Mending Basket

Bless the Lord, O my soul;
and all that is within me,
bless his holy name...
Who redeems your life from the pit;
who crowns you with lovingkindness
and compassion.
Psalm 103:1,4

This is a mending kind of day. The October sun has reached into golden, red, and brown-tinged trees, and I can hear the soft sound of glory around me.

Walking among crunchy, just-fallen leaves, I rejoice in seeing brightly colored birds at the back porch feeder. I fold freshblown sheets from the clothesline and think how balmy the windwhipped air is.

I laugh as the dog rolls in the grass at my feet, covering her ears at the burst of my song. There's great fun in watching squirrels leap from red dogwood limbs to hideaway hemlock branches. Even the withering vegetable vines speak peace in this softened, coming-to-winter day.

In the quiet of a house where footsteps

and voices are momentarily stilled, I can listen to violins or favorite Broadway musicals on the stereo. Or I can just sit and soak up the silence.

The clamor of voices demanding laundry, meals, money, decisions, meetings, and schedules are all shut away from this gifted time of solitude.

My heart is capable again, after this rest. I can welcome the sounds of children, the ring of the telephone, and the appearance of appointment lists on the bulletin board.

Lord, after this—the morning of singing at my work, the noontime of reading alone, the afternoon of woods-walking—I am whole and available again.

Thank you, loving Lord, for the careful mending of my tattered spirit, this peaceful autumn day.

Darning Thread

Lord, at the time when I'm needed the most,
I'm falling apart.
Like the sweater I'm mending,
All the threads have become frayed
At the point where I wear them the most,
And there is a gaping hole.

The soft lavender thread of peace is broken
 harshly;
That yellow joy-yarn seems to have thinned
 to nothing;
The red laughter-and-fun one has been cut,
And is raveling back into the fabric
So that griping and complaining are filling
The place where it used to be.
Even the cool green of song has shredded
And disappeared.

I can't gather up these ends and make them
 strong again;
They are forever broken—
But the heavy darning thread of your love
Never thins or frays
Or ravels at the edges.

Sew me up, Lord;
Bind me together again,

So that the rubbed place
Where I've been too much used
Can be stronger than ever.

Over the spot where there was nothing
But tattered, ragged ends,
Make a smooth, safe place
For leaning and holding on.

With the needle of forgiveness and love
Mend the person I was going to be;
Make me into the mother you see
In the perfection of your pattern book.

Divorce Tangle

And my God shall supply all your needs according to his riches in glory in Christ Jesus.
Philippians 4:19

I was fumbling in the kitchen drawer for a ball of twine when the telephone rang and I heard my friend sobbing. Her husband had finally left, and she was facing the destruction of a divorce.

This is a precious Christian woman. For months now she has suffered, knowing the marriage was over, but hoping and praying for a miracle, a solution, a renewal of vows made long ago before God. She wants to do the right thing and that includes honoring those promises.

Today, all hope is gone with her husband. Soon he will be free to marry the other woman, but what will my friend's freedom mean to her? Aside from the terrible recognition that years of promise and commitment are invalid, she has to recover somehow from the devastating blow to her self-esteem caused by this ultimate rejection and cope with overwhelming personal, physical and emotional needs.

Then there are her three children. What will happen to them, to their need for two loving parents, a family, rules to live by, faith, to their ideals for marriage? Will they ever trust anybody again? Will she be strong enough to influence them for good, though the man she and they love has deserted them, breaking all of his promises?

How will she manage financially? What happens when the house needs paint, or the children need a doctor, or the bills mount up? Where does she turn when she desperately needs someone to hold her and listen to the tragedies of her day? Will *she* ever trust anyone again? Will she be able to trust God? What on earth can I do to help her?

I'm frustrated. It's happening everywhere, in the church as well as outside. No family is immune from the horrible disease of divorce. I don't know where to turn for help.

Suddenly, among pencils, coupons, birthday candles, and old batteries, there is the ball of string. In a flash of memory I see my father's large expressive hands working patiently with knots and tangles in string salvaged from packages and assorted scavenging. Untangling it looked impossible to me as a child, making finally a neatly wrapped ball of string for our family's use.

So, Lord, your patient, loving, capable fingers can untangle this mess of my friend's life. Her children, the other woman's children, the other husband—where does it all end? Where is any healing for them? It takes faith to entrust this handful of broken, tangled loyalties and lives to you and leave it alone. By that same faith, though, I can see all the strings of my friend's life perfect and secure, wrapped neatly like that ball of twine. I trust your Word that all her needs can be supplied according to your riches in glory by Christ Jesus.

Upswing

Playground-sand beneath my feet slips away.
I feel again, as in a thrill of memory,
The surge and flip of something
   inside my self.
The swing soars into the sky and
Abruptly
Down again.

Above the spring-heavy green of
   dogwood bough,
Into the piled-on blue of heaven,
My soul takes instant flight.
From deep inside the song thrusts up:
"There has to be a God!"
There can be no beauty, no haunting melody,
No freedom in the eternity of blue,
No forgiveness in the eyes of my
   growing-up one,
No small fingers wrapping 'round my heart,
No tears that come in answer to my prayer.

Until, searching, I find
Winged, fulfilling Joy,
Protecting Presence,
Love come swooping down
From God Who is.

First Flight

*Let me dwell in your tent forever;
Let me take refuge
in the shelter of your wings.
Psalm 61:4*

Why is it that a big, huffing, growling bus can cause this heaviness inside me?

Why, suddenly, are those tears so close to the surface? In the chill morning air, I sniff the atmosphere of the children's excitement, mixed with exhaust fumes from the waiting vehicles.

My firstborn, with a quick, pointedly casual "Bye, Mom," is off. Pillow under one arm and an instrument under the other, she joins her friends for this first longed-for band trip.

As the procession rolls out of the school driveway, my tears flow unashamedly. I want to go with her.

In a few years, she'll be gone from home. I won't be able to share her trials and triumphs as I do now. This afternoon, during supper preparation, I'll envision her proudly carrying out the routine she's worked days and hours on end to perfect. And tonight, in the wee hours, I'll listen to the overflow of excitement, the thrills and funny mistakes, and how "We just died laughing."

Lord, not long ago she was little, and I was a part of all her happy and sad times. Now, she's moving away into her world. She has to make that world. She has to approve or change it.

I have to wait and listen and be grateful for the love she shares in a telephone call, when "We won Mom! I love you!" interrupts my long winter's nap.

So put me together, Lord—all new—to be the mother my flying teenager needs.

And thank you, Lord, for her strong wings.

Mother's Window

All the oak leaves are brown now,
Hovering
Against the coming chill.
The scarlet bird comes to feed
At the barren maple's box.

Sunlight slides under ruffled panels,
Across purple winter violets
And spills on the round red rug,
Where the cat curls,
And licks,
And settles to sleep.

I am surrounded by quiet
Until the school bus comes.

The Pondering

*But Mary treasured up all these things,
pondering them in her heart.*
Luke 2:19

What a frightful rush I was in that day at school! I was late picking up the children for a doctor's appointment; Mary wanted to show me her latest art work; and Jim was still on hall patrol. It was beginning to feel like one of those hectic, disorganized dreams I sometimes have.

At first when a teacher stopped me, I wanted to run. She and I had already had some "little talks" during the year. But her face, even at the end of a long school day, was shining!

"I just have to tell you," she said, "how very much I have enjoyed having Jim in my class lately. He's behaving very well and doing good work."

"My Jim?" I sputtered stupidly, thinking, *the one who has only "dumb old teachers," and a lot of "stupid homework"?*

She hurried off and I stood looking after her, open-mouthed and unbelieving. That same son had been at the top of my prayer list just last week. I had begun to be frightened by his ten-year old disposition, and I had asked the Lord to help him subdue his temper and gain some self-control.

Lord, now I remember. Even as I hold this small treasure and warm it near my heart, I am ashamed. I am so late and so lacking in my gratitude.

Thank you Lord, that you always hear me, though I may have forgotten the prayer. You always answer me, even after I've begun worrying about something else.

Breakfast Miracle

*And be kind to one another, tender-hearted,
forgiving each other, just as God in Christ
also has forgiven you.*
Ephesians 4:32

Last night, when the supper I had cooked for the family lay in ruins, and the dining room was filled with echoes of parents and children yelling at each other, I cried out for help. "These children have a good father, and I'm afraid they're going to grow up never knowing it!"

My greatest concern was for Jerry's relationship with his teenage girls. When the shouting started it was because their kid brother Tim did something dumb like spilling the gravy, and Julie corrected him rather ungraciously. Then their dad got into it and the girls finally left the table in tears. Feeling helpless, wrongly accused, and angry, they slammed off to their rooms. Of course I was in there too, trying to take both sides and making matters worse. Our whole evening together was smashed in pieces. Suddenly nobody wanted to live here, especially me. I was left with dirty dishes and a despairing heart.

"I know Jerry's explosion came because there is so much over-work and stress in his job right now," I sniffled into the snowy suds, *"but why can't this home be a haven for him and a nurturing place for the children? Why can't we love one another? We're supposed to be a Christian family, after all."* I didn't even know what to pray for. It would take a miracle, and we certainly didn't deserve that!

But a miracle is what happened at breakfast this morning!

As Julie slunk past her dad, I saw him turn and put his arms around her saying, "Sugar, please forgive me for yelling at you last night. I do love you so much."

I was crying into the pancake batter as I watched her return the hug and nod her head. A smile shone through her tears.

Then, when I heard Julie's kind words to Tim, I had to leave the room. Imagine her offering to pour him extra juice instead of the usual, "Leave some for the rest of us, you pig!" Tim was so happy that he was nice to Mary, who came in all unawares and didn't know what to say to anybody!

It was like a chain reaction, begun with one act of love and forgiveness. Suddenly the unhappy shouting was gone, replaced by laughter and chatter.

Lord, these children do have a good father, and I think they know it! But Lord, couldn't we just have this love-stuff around all the time? Never mind, Lord. If we didn't live through the rough, shouting, angry times, we'd never learn about forgiveness and how good love feels in a family.

Laundry Room

Praise the Lord, all nations;
Laud him, all peoples!
For his lovingkindness is great toward us,
And the truth of the Lord is everlasting.
Praise the Lord!

Psalm 117

It's morning, and here we are again—me and the washing machine. Once more I'm sorting soggy, smelly sheets, socks, and pajamas. The rain steaks my window and the dryer's been acting funny lately.

I begin every day by stripping the same bed, turning the same socks, picking up the same wet towels, and loading the same machines. This morning I am really resenting that.

I'm such a good, hardworking mother. How can this happen to me over and over again? Is that child going to college in diapers? Are the others never going to learn to pick up after themselves?

The worst of it all is that the washing machine mocks me! It sings, swishing back and forth in a familiar rhythm, and I find myself humming along with it. The words the children sang last Sunday are rolling like praise off my tongue.

> Praise the Lord in the wind and sunshine;
> Praise the Lord in the dark of night,
> Praise the Lord in the rain or snow
> Or in the morning light.[1]

The words just fit in the sunshine-filled church, with the glory of little children in spotless choir robes, their hair only slightly out of place. But now? Should I praise the Lord for a bed-wetter, a thoughtless teenager, argumentative siblings, dark stormy mornings, and appliances that break down?

> Praise the Lord in the time of sorrow,
> Praise the Lord in the time of joy.
> Praise the Lord every moment,
> Nothing let your praise destroy![1]

Oh! that's when praise works best, doesn't it Lord? In the dark of night praise is the only answer to resentment, depression, and undeserved hurt.

Like the fresh, clean wash I take from the machine, my spirit is cleansed by praise, and I don't really need a reason for this song. I am praising a God who IS. You are nearer than the

---

[1] Natalie Sleeth, "Praise the Lord" (Chapel Hill, NC: Hinshaw Music, Inc., 1985). Reprinted by permission.

anger and discouragement, because you want to be!

"Hallelujah" is the only word that fits the rhythm of your constant, understanding love. It pushes the other sounds away; there's no room for anything but praise.

Blurred Vision

*For now we see in a mirror dimly,
but then face to face;
now I know in part,
but then shall I know fully
just as I also have been fully known.*
1 Corinthians 13:12

These bifocals *are* helping me! After the first depressing days of admitting age and infirmity are creeping up on me, of sweeping floors that insisted on coming up to meet me, of stumbling over things that weren't there, and of groping up and down steps, I *can see* my world better around that little blurry line.

The discomfort that always came from not being able to read and sew, fit tiny screws into tiny holes, remove a splinter from a child's finger, or thread a needle without a youngster's condescending help, is gone.

As I read the familiar closing words of the "Corinthian love chapter," I think I'm learning something. Paul says that, just as I need help to see with my physical eyes, so my spiritual vision is clouded and imperfect.

There is so much I don't understand, so much that's blurred and dim.

It occurs to me, Lord, that I need to see you "through a glass, darkly," because I just couldn't bear the brightness with these earthly eyes, this untrained spiritual vision.

But I can imagine the joy when I see you face to face! I won't need bifocals (or even dark glasses for protection) to behold the glory I can only dimly imagine today. Everything I enjoy in your world is only a dingy phantom of the beauty you have in store for me in heaven.

One day, there will be no more groping, stumbling, depression, or frustration. There will be no reason to say, "I don't understand," because I will see and know, "even as I am known."

Hallelujah, Lord! I can hardly wait. In the meantime, I do appreciate these new bifocals.

Dangerous Roar

*Be sober, be vigilant,
because your adversary the devil,
as a roaring lion,
walks about seeking whom he may devour.*
1 Peter 5:8

This beautiful, warm, early-fall school day is still sparkling, but I am weary and much wiser than a few hours ago. When we came outdoors this morning, the kindergarten children had such fun rolling on the carpet-like lawn. Their excitement at being alive and healthy was almost drowned out by the roar of a giant earth-moving machine just across the busy road where a shopping center is going up.

The other teachers and I chatted and enjoyed the sun and children's laughter. Then, suddenly, three-year-old Jeffrey ran as fast as his short legs and inquisitive mind could take him, straight toward that road. For a heart-stopping instant I was frozen with fear.

Then calmly, so as not to frighten him, I

called, "Jeffrey, let's come back here and play."

So intent was he on the drama before him, he didn't hear. As quietly as possible and breathing a prayer all the way, I strode toward him, reaching him just before he slid into the ditch which separated the grassy area from the treacherous highway.

My knees would hardly support me as I picked up his squirming body, carried him back to safety, and scolded him about leaving the play area. I knew he couldn't understand the fear I felt as I visualized his limp, broken body on that road. His world had always been safe and protected.

Lord, I'm so much like Jeffrey. I enjoy the freedom you give me in your beautiful world. There is sunshine and protection where you are.

But there is always danger. The harmful effects of sin are waiting on the other side of the partially concealed ditch. I am warned in scripture, by the admonitions of fellow Christians, and by a voice within. If I am determined to keep going after the thing that entices me, ignoring the warning calls of danger, there is a terrible price to pay.

I know that my concern for Jeffrey's safety is nothing compared to the great love you have for me. I may not like the scolding, but I am grateful for the protection, Lord.

Visiting Day

I was in prison, and you came unto me.
Matthew 25:36

The chill December rain streaked across my kitchen window. I finished putting away the last of the Sunday dinner dishes and looked longingly at the family sprawled in front of the living-room's warm fire.

"Who wants to go out in this?" I grumbled as I shrugged into a raincoat and picked up the box of food and gifts I had prepared for my friend.

Rainy or not, this was the day for my visit to the Women's Correctional Center. My prisoner friend's family lived far away and she was looking forward to seeing me at this holiday time.

After I drove across town, and was admitted to the Center's reception room, my carefully prepared packages were taken away and were inspected. Along with other visitors, many of them families with small children, I was brusquely checked and escorted to the huge assembly hall which served as a visitor's center. After being shown to a chair, I waited for my friend to be brought by a guard. As I looked around, anger at the treatment I had received was replaced by a real sorrow for the people there.

This was no place to share family relationships. How could anyone bring cheer to the drab lives of these inmates? But this was the only place they had. Sweethearts, friends, husbands and wives, parents and children, were trying to keep alive the fragile bond which had been shattered by whatever crime had caused this separation.

My friend, dressed in a green prison uniform, was smiling as she approached. It was natural to greet her with an embrace, even though we had seen each other rarely in the past two years since we became "pen pals."

For thirty minutes, we chatted about our families, classes she was taking, projects she was involved in, and what God had done for her, even in this place. It was exciting to hear that for the first time in five years, there was the possibility of work release and then parole. In a few weeks, she might actually step outside these secured gates.

All too soon a guard tapped her on her shoulder and I knew our time was up. We embraced again, promising to pray for one another, and I watched as she took her place in a line to be marched back to the dormitory.

Lord Jesus, this place needs your compassion. How many of these women, like my friend, wouldn't even be here if someone had shared the story of your love with them?

My heart is breaking for the families—children with large wondering eyes being snatched away from young mothers; a teenage girl holding tentatively to a sweet-faced woman in green; beautiful, promising young women meeting their pimps here, because that's the only life they know; a young husband pulling his chair close to his weeping wife, trying to hold her; aging parents with determined smiles on lined, weary-eyed faces, saying goodbye.

If these tug at my heart, what do they do to you, Lord? You made them all for your glory and they are so lost. There is the glimmer of hope in my friend who has taken advantage of the Bible studies and self-help programs offered by church and community groups here. But her family, like the others, is also paying a "debt to society." I know you love them too, Lord, and I pray for each one as they come through all that official "security," for a glimpse of the one they love in this crowded, inhuman place.

The message of Christmas is almost desperate here. As I leave, I notice on the reception room wall a mural of the Nativity. Do they know you are the babe there, Lord? Do they have any idea how much love you would pour out on them, this month and all year? Your love can overcome the fear and despair that reigns in this place. My friend and I are praying for that too, as we remember each other.

Thank you, Lord, for sending me out in this December drizzle, to celebrate Christmas.

Reclaimed

A gleaming, useful vessel,
Lord, for you?
This earthen crock—
Lip cracked, sides chipped and stained,
Deep dust of years inside,
Lost in the pantry corner and forgotten—
Gleaming, Lord?
Useful? Me, Lord?
Can you repair this old clay pot?

It's not comfortable, Lord—
This awful-tasting glue,
The painful beating of my sides,
This frightening filling-up feeling.
Does it take all this, Lord,
For me to come out of the
Comfortable, quiet, useless
Place I've been,
And blink to see
Your glory reflected in me?

More Than Enough

Therefore you are no longer a slave, but a son; and if a son, then an heir through God.
Galatians 4:7

All week long, it had been like holding the reins of wild horses. Now Julie had finished washing the bathroom window and was asking, "Do I have to do anything else?" Then she was gone, riding her bicycle down the street to her friend's house.

All four children were home from school. "Spring break," they called it. But it was no "break" for me. I had planned their chores carefully, window-washing, floor-waxing, closet-cleaning, trying to keep them busy and avoid the squabbles that come from boredom. I also wanted them to help me get the spring cleaning done. Why shouldn't they help? They were healthy and finally old enough to be really useful around here.

But I had forgotten about the plans that are made in preparation for a week out of school. All Sunday afternoon the telephone rang. Activities ranged from picnics to swim parties, to sleepovers both here at home and away.

Monday morning, however, I held to my original edict: "No playing until the assigned jobs are done."

Grudgingly, they lined up to see what was on the list, and each one checked off his work as it was completed. That sounds easy. It wasn't! As any mother knows, it would have been simpler to do it all myself. Complaints and sibling arguments filled the air, and the telephone conversations described slaves kept in their own house, while "everyone else" had a vacation.

Lord, I've had that same attitude sometimes. So have many of your children down through the ages. My children are not slaves and neither am I.

I am your precious child. It is my privilege to come as Julie and the others have been known to do occasionally and ask, "What can I do to help?" That's when it is good, Lord. We can work together to clean house, feed the poor, teach church school, or do whatever jobs you have for us because we love you.

It is nice to have a clean house, but it's much nicer to have a child come and offer to help with supper.

Now, what can I do for you, Lord?

Constant Reminder

*Behold I have inscribed you
on the palms of my hands....*
Isaiah 49:16

It was a strange sight. As I walked out of the church last Sunday, I noticed our minister writing on his hand. He seemed to be engrossed in conversation with a newcomer, and apparently had nothing else on which to write an address or whatever was so important about the lady. So he simply wrote her name and other information on the palm of his hand until he could get to the study and his little black book.

Whenever our pastor used his hand for anything that day, he would see the reminder of that person. She would be near to him and his thoughts for several hours.

But Lord, you say that my name is tattooed on your hands! That means it won't come off! I can't get much closer than that, or more permanently remembered. This makes me feel cherished and important. You love me enough to keep me close, to write me into your hand, so that I cannot be lost or forgotten.

What wonderful love it is that binds me to my Lord like this! Help me, Lord, to remember my tattooed name, even when I think I'm too busy, or too confused, or too angry to be close to you.